Conversations With My Higher Self

Praise for Conversations With My Higher Self

To walk outside your own body. To look back and see yourself as the universe sees you. To see the entire story of your life laid open before you and to thumb through it page by page and truly understand. To see clearly, all the events that have lead up to where you are now and the choices you made, actions you took, and to gain a snapshot of your soul.

Pain, loss, joy, grief, death, and rebirth. To know that you have done it all the best you were able and that above all else you survived. And love, the greatest of all emotions, is within you. You are loved, you have loved, and you deserve love.

Most of all the deepest love possible.

To love yourself.

What would the scenario described above look like? If anyone is capable of drawing out a sketch of these events, I believe Rachel Finch is just such a person.

She has painted a deeply emotional picture of this landscape and through her eyes we are able to gain a rare glimpse into what it might be like to view yourself from afar.

In *Conversations With My Higher Self*, Finch takes us on a guided tour of self-perception from outside one's psyche. It's a marvellous journey of exploration and discussion with one's own consciousness.

Asking difficult questions and receiving difficult answers, as only your own heart can give.

I was profoundly moved by this piece. As a poet and an empathic soul, my heart and mind were solidly gripped by the experience of reading this book.

If you are one who enjoys philosophical discussions about how the events in your life have molded you into the person you are, then this is exactly the book for you.

It will leave you with a profound feeling of having witnessed something beautiful.

It will also likely uncover the hidden answers in your mind to some of the most desperate questions your heart has been asking.

-Eric Sydal, author of *Pantheon*

Rachel Finch's *Conversations With My Higher Self* is brilliant and beautiful. Rachel reaches into the depth of her soul to share the journey of her time in the afterlife.

From the first page to the last word, I became immersed in her words. My heart broke when I read about her leaving her body. I felt my chest would burst with love from her time in the light. I wept when she struggled when life was breathed back into her. I smiled at the end because of her courage to share her journey with the world.

I never thought a book would impact me the way *Conversations With My Higher Self* did. Rachel's journey has changed me in a way, a beautiful way. You will have a new understanding of life and death once you read *Conversations With My Higher Self.*

For me, *Conversations With My Higher Self* gives the answer to the question is there life after death. Rachel does this by giving us a glimpse of what is on the other side-transformation, light and love.

"I am outside of myself,
more whole without shape and
I exist as a spectra of light,
nebula shining bright,
I am matter
and more."

-April Y. Spellmeyer, author of *Sacrifice & Bloom*

Conversations with My Higher Self is a provocative book and certainly a deeply moving and unique one. If you are expecting a book with overused themes, themes that tend to dominate social media and modern poetry books, this is not that book. It's clever, it's honest, it's spiritual, it's cathartic, it's a modern-day masterpiece.

"The ceiling disappears beneath my feet as I rise up." *CWMHS* is Finch's personal experience with a near death, out-of-body life-changing event. Not only does she have the power to create such vivid imagery that you feel as though you are in the room with her, Finch had a way of carrying me with her to that other place outside our physical bodies, that place we can't possibly see with human eyes, to that spiritual realm beyond.

"I am a god dressed in skin, fully aware of my otherworldliness and I am lonely, so terribly lonely, my own kind, lost in an amnesia I have left behind and I am craving home."

This book is a book like none you've read before and that alone is a powerful testament to Finch's artistic brilliance. She executes her near death and resurrection experiences in such a way as to bring the reader with her to this incredible other-world. As Finch evolves, I felt myself evolving. "She is not quiet, the evolving is an unfolding and I am origami in the wind." *CWMHS* has the power to change you, the reader, to change your mindset and see yourself and your life in an entirely different light. This book is a must have for all lovers of poetry and anyone who has had or who has known someone with a near death and out-of-body experience.

-Melody Lee, author of Moon Gypsy, and Season of the Sorceress

Also by Rachel Finch

A Sparrow Stirs its Wings

They think I'm lost
inside my head, but
I am nowhere close.

I am light years away
in a sky that folds
to my bend, that
moulds itself into me
and I am levitating in
a paradise of
constellation castles.

Conversations With My Higher Self

Rachel Finch

Conversations With My Higher Self
Copyright ©2019 Rachel Finch

Published in the United States of America by Indie Blu(e)
Publishing

ISBN 978-1-7328000-5-2
Library of Congress Control Number: 2019941504

Editors: Christine E. Ray
                   Kindra M. Austin
Cover Design & Interior Artwork:
                   Amanda Coleman

Dedication

To the light.
To Demi.

For Scott. For Willow.

I want my heart to swell so big
when it ceases to beat, it explodes
all the love I built, ten thousand
miles in each direction.

For Carter

I first met Love when I was
out of body, Love
became me.
Light seeped into whatever I was
without form and filled
every part of me until I burst.

You can burst from Love you know,
but it doesn't obliterate you,
it expands you and you become
Light.

For Joanna

I want to package what it feels like to fly,
in a chestnut box, with golden ribbon and
watch my sister's face when she opens it
and hears the angels singing.

Table of Contents

Out of Body

I am tense, my bones are heavy within my skin,
my hands, stiff, try and move to brush against my outer
but they are icy and it feels like I am pinching myself.

The ward is dull, a ghostly mist resting itself around me,
I am confused, I can't remember what warmth is.
My body is shuddering and I'm acutely aware that
my jaw is a machine in motion and I scold myself,
trying to remember if it's me or the bone in control and I'm
wondering if my teeth will
shatter from the force.

I stretch out an arm, fumbling for the biggest red orb that
suddenly seems so small, lost in the mountain of one thin
sheet
bundled beside me, my fingers are long dark branches and the
trunk of me buckles beneath the weight of this movement.

I am abruptly surrounded, looking expectantly for armfuls of
blankets
that are not there
and I am a jumble of questions that cannot form.
I am only thinking.

I question if I can be seen.
A rainbow of women crowd my bed, all faces staring into the
one
plastered all over Me and yet I don't feel visible.
I am looking for the warmth, but the piercing white of their
uniforms is
blinding and I try and look anywhere but here.

They tell me to sit, I half haul my limp figure higher in the
bed and
I am seething, trying to drag myself, up a snowy mountain
that
doesn't care for footprints and
I am sliding,
other peoples' arms beneath mine, steel rods that burn at the
touch
and I imagine freezing in this moment, I imagine the frost
creeping
from my fingertips into theirs, if they'll feel the bite.

My eyes trace the interlocking of our limbs, I see my hands,
reaching
in their stillness and I notice that my fingers are turning blue.
My neck moves the crown of me, there is no thought,
I am tilted, counting 8, 9, 10 little
lagoons forming at the tips of my fingers and I want to
swim for eons.

My eyes are frantic, I don't know what I'm looking for,
a hundred foreign hands grab at my structure, a needle
pierces my skin, a dagger crushing a hundred layers of
solid ice beneath my flesh and I am screaming a silent scream
that reverberates in my ears only and
I am unhinged.

One woman, or three, forces a mask onto my face
and I can't make theirs out anymore,
I am locked in a prison, choking on my own breath and
I ask myself if I am dying.

My psyche vibrates, *calm*

and I am swimming in a word.

I lay back just a little and I am
sinking a mile deep into myself.
I can see their lips moving, but I am a
million light years from their bodies,
the sound of their voices, a faint whisper in
the distance and I focus on the gentle rhythm of
the beat within my chest.

Mostly, there are no words, but when I hear them
they repeat,
duplicate and deafen me.

They are calling for my people,
but my people are too far
and I am drenched in solitude.

Baby girl on my right,
doesn't see me reaching, doesn't hear
my heart pierce the room,
let me take her.

I am looking for an entry point,
scanning my arm, an innocuous
pore winking red, I am conscious,
thinking, no man would see this
wound if he did not know it, no
man would see this poison
flowing through my bloodstream
if it did not steal the colour
from my cheekbones.

Rachel Finch

Time has slowed and I am
watching it form before,
as, after
and I am suspended in
a moment with split vision
and I am inside of myself looking
out and outside of myself looking
in and my selves are parallel.

I am hovering in a moment of
uncertainty and knowing
and it is an eternal understanding.

The slow closing of my eyelids, is a
gentle goodbye.
I imagine my lashes blowing
kisses to all the hearts that touched my life
while my eyes roll backward and my lips
part, so I may escape myself.

My heart rate is dropping,
tired eyes fixated on the ocean creeping into my
skin,
Voice behind my eyelids introduces
itself,

Slowly,
slowly,
10, 9,
everything's okay,
everything's okay,
8, 7,
this body is ready,
this body is ready,
6, 5,
easy breaths,
easy breaths,
4, 3,
remember who you are,
remember who you are,
2, 1,
up,
up, and
I remember.

I hover over her for the longest time,
unable to comprehend my own position in this place,
she is sleeping but I know she hears me.
I am aware of a room full of people that don't seem to be
aware of
me
and I am perplexed.
I look at her heavy head of hair and imagine what it feels like
to
touch it.
I reach out, but I move right through her and in my confusion
I turn to stare
at myself.

There is a voice that is whispering to me from within and I am trying to establish who it is.

I am outside of myself,
more whole without shape and
I exist as a spectra of light,
nebula shining bright,
I am matter
and more.

For a thousand years,
I stare at her face.
I memorise every pore on
her skin, creep inside each one,
nestle the memory of me into
her bones and hope
she remembers.

The ceiling disappears beneath my feet as I
rise up.
I am losing track of time and
space and
my present shape and I am
flailing upside down in a vast expanse that tastes like
déjà vu but I can't place the
flavour.

My vision is clear and I am
observing everything I can only
glimpse in the
tumble.
Darkness engulfs me, yet all is
illuminated and I am
wondering if candlelight is witnessing my
upward skydive.

I see the sphere of soil and water
below me,
ebbing out like the tide.
I can't tell if it is spinning or if
I am.

The speed with which I'm moving
transports me back in
time and I am ten years old on a
rollercoaster ride and I am
smiling, ear to ear.

It feels like wind is rushing through me,
I feel like I have my mouth wide open
and the gale is filling my throat, but
I have become aware, my mouth and throat are
elsewhere and I can't see what I look like anymore.

I let go of my before and think to face ahead,
I do not turn, it just is and I am facing a whole new
direction.
I am in a dark, translucent tunnel, a thin veil of film
separating me from the vastness and I am aware of
other beings.
I think to myself, *who are they* and a quiet voice
within me murmurs,
they are you.
I am startled at the thought I think
without thinking it and before a question forms it is
answered and I am aware of her within me.

She is a little behind the outer layer of me,
as if I had been split in two through the
crown
of my head and our pieces just fit back together after a
lifetime
of detachment.

I have stepped outside of myself and I am
all thought.
Alone, in the presence of me and
myself and
I.
I am flying, weightless, I look for
wings.
I am trying to catch a breath I cannot grasp,
I do not need,
no part of me is hollow,
I am free.

Our surroundings have altered and I feel
shielded.
We are no longer travelling and I am in a
room with no walls.
My entire visual perception is focused on
all that surrounds me, a single crystalline screen
that stretches outside of all else.
I am wrapped in a blessed moment and
unaware of any existence outside of this.

The images are flickering and again I look for
tiny flames, wondering what light is causing the glow.

I hear her giggle and she beckons; I face her and
I look inside myself and am
awestruck at the sight,
she is the light.

I think back to the sound of my voice but
I can't remember how to form a syllable or
any tone other than this warm vibration,
an eternal echo of my beginning and
I'm not sure where I am.

I am present with myself beside me,
we are travelling and I am tumbling
upward.

I ask myself if I am flying,
I answer myself,
you are being called home
and I don't have time
to recall because time is
a memory hurrying behind me
and we are wanted somewhere else.

We slow to a still and I am present in a
sacred moment,
I am observing and
reliving.

I am simultaneous.

Ahead of me, I see myself,
born, small, a little bigger,
a billion versions of me
existing in a second that
refuses to be defined
as a second and I am
meeting parts of myself I had
misplaced,
buried,
remembered,
despised and
loved.

I am an ocean and I am
drowning
in my own deep feeling.

I want to look away but I am
everywhere,
little voice whispers,
it is as it should be and now you know.

We spend an eternity,
merging into
each other,
staring at ourselves,
in a thousand mirrors,
each face speaking in
a different tongue and
as I go from then to now and
there to here and
her to me,
I learn every language I never knew
lived within me.

And when every word that ever existed rests
within my psyche, she tells me stories
without any words
and I finally remember
how spirit speaks.

Rachel Finch

I am watching myself dancing,
the vision in front of me,
myself split into four hundred honeycombs,
pirouetting on every prism,
my laughter is a travelling echo
and I am eating joy by the spoonful.

She tells me,
slowly.
She tells me,
it's okay.
She tells me,
you are Loved.
What have you learned?
And the movie of my life starts to play.

The little girl I am seeing is not familiar
for the longest time.
I am watching a million moments,
in unison and I am
lost in my memories.

She tells me,
pause
and the movie is gone.

I am in
my body on my father's shoulders
and we are spinning. I am
overcome with joy, I am elated to
feel this, it is brief and everlasting and she tells me,
go.

I am zooming through years and again we
slow.
I am watching five hundred
balloons float to the sky and I can't take my eyes off
the clouds.

I am running with my sister, chasing her and she is

laughing and every fibre of my being is alive with that
sound
and I feel my
second self delight in this treasure.

I am seven years old, unfamiliar hands in my knickers and
I am choking on my own pungent shame.
She embraces me.

I am seventeen years old, blade against my skin,
praying for my own death.
She embraces me.

I am reliving every moment my heart ever
beat me through and I am
lying in the hospital ward with half the blood I
started with.
She embraces me.

She tells me,
slowly.
She tells me,
it's okay.
She tells me,
you are Loved.
What have you learnt?
And we are moving.

I can taste shame
all the way from my
gut to my tongue
but I have no lips
to spit the flavour
and there's nowhere
to look but this
space within myself
that never knew itself
like it could have.

I am four feet tall,
horizontal in my bed,
half asleep,
rising, moving through
the wall and I am
floating.
I am mesmerised by
the street lamps for
an age. I am a moth
searching for a flame
and I am travelling.

I know the route, I
walk it all the time with
my earth mother but
she's not with me now
and the hill looks
really long and steep.
I know I'm roaming far
from home, but I don't
mind because I know
where I am headed
when he stops me.

Man with his hand on my
shoulder. Man that I know
but will forget. Man made of
light like me, gently turning me,
carefully reminding me,
it's too far, not yet,
mind your cord.

I look down and the ribbon

from my navel looks like
a river of silver and I look
back to where I was headed
and I am all wonder.

In this space, I know each star by name,
I house every memory ever made and
I am high, looking
below me,
beside me,
above me and
all I see is
everything.

In this knowing,
there are memories
from many lives
and I am remembering
choosing the mother,
choosing the womb,
choosing the milk.
I am remembering
the ageing of my skin,
the breathless deaths
and every flight.

Remembering the knowing of
her
is reverence.

I am seven years old,
high above my body
and she guides me.

Away from the pain
between my legs, I am
flying, we are surrounded
by other beings as
small as me and we are
bouncing on a castle
in the sky.

I had forgotten this place,
this delight, this journey
I made every night and
out of body I remember
and keep the recollection.

I am spinning,
dispersing into fragments,
but I have forgotten separateness.
It is easy to be, or not be,
to form or to scatter and
I allow us.

I look for her, she is now
only sound,
tucked into the deepest layer of me and
she tells me,
fly.

It is instant, this rushing that
thrusts through me,
this need and knowing to
glide
and I don't need directions.

She is launching me forward from
within myself and I am staring far ahead,
searching.
I can feel her excitement,
she is eager.
Her sense ripples through me and I
remember exultation.

Every fibre of my being is throbbing,
my essence pulsing for this moment,
her rejoicing drumming at my core and
I finally see it.

I can taste our smile when I make out the
Little Light
and she tells me
faster.
I am shooting at an unfathomable speed,
I am the air and she squeals,
now.

The warmth fills me far from the target,
I can feel myself sinking into it and
I am dissolving.

We burst through the veil, I hear her glee,
wings
and I am
motionless.

Hovering in this sphere of light, I am in
ecstasy.

The presence of Love astounds me.

I am floating, all feelings of fear have
escaped me and I cease to exist in any
space other than here.

Light is bursting into me, purity
penetrating my being and I am aware,
a fountain of iridescence raining
down upon me, in this pause,
I become.

I am in euphoria.
Suspended in a light of
nothingness that is
everything and I am pure emotion.

This moment is eternal and I am
transfixed. My thoughts are
fleeting, intoxicating, I am
struck continually with
light beams of a Love that
overwhelms me and everything that
ever was is whole.

She is no longer a part of me,
she is all of me and we are all
of the light that becomes us.

And I am aware.

Of what is present and what
is not.
That pain and shame,
have been banished from me, that
fear was never real, you are home.

I am thinking thoughts that
aren't mine again
and it becomes clear they belong to
all that is
and I am all gratitude.

I hover in a grief and a welcome and a
rapture.
I am a bird and a whale and a lion and
synchronously I am none of these things.

Much is explained to me in this
mother tongue and I want to stay draped
in this moment
eternally.

All I hear is singing and I am
enveloped in this sound.
I am frozen in time,
birth,
death,
rebirth,
eternity and the bliss is
enormous.

I am in the presence of the gods,
but they don't look like gods,
they look like
love and
light,
crystals and
magic,
honey and
shooting stars and I am lost for
every word I ever needed and
no longer need.

My senses are lessened a little, the
silent conversation is louder, I'm trying to
stay focused on the paradise.
I don't want to talk, only
be,
enveloped but there is a dull
urgency and I force myself to shift
my attention to the message.

I am asked,
do you wish to go back?
I am horror-struck,
hurt,
at the thought and in an
instant, I cry out,
No.
This is my Soul at full volume.

There is a pause and
I am asked again,
do you wish to go back?
And every layer of me is
remembering,
reliving the movie and I am screaming,
No.

I am shown a moment in time that I
am not present in.
I am looking at the baby with the full
head of hair and I know her.

And I know her.

My Soul exhales, a deep, knowing sigh,
no doubt in my psyche and l say
Yes.

I state that I do not wish to be alone,
that the alone, is an army of daggers that
slice and I am told, I never will be,
I never was.
I am all trust.

Chorus of angels,
sings to me,
the lyrics,
I love you,
in a thousand voices I never knew I knew,
a song that sews itself into me,
that will never end.

I ask for a moment more and it is
granted and I am
relishing in Love for as long as
I can and I am taking it back with me.

Love is a river
flowing,
roaring,
breathing and
I am swimming
underwater in
its movement.

Love is a seashell
and I am the sound.

I am sucked backward,
so fast I can barely process,
I am as cold as ice,
I am light years from home,
I am solid grief.

Rachel Finch

Resurrection

I thud back into my body,
heavy
and empty,
cold to my core,
grieving who I thought
I was and I am searching for the
singing I have been denied.

A gentle hum, vibrates through me,
someone else's blood coursing through my veins,
and I can't tell if I am remembering their dreams
or my own.

My body shakes to the beat of
a non-existent sob and I wonder if I left it
in the sky.

I can hear voices in the distance,
they are so loud I can taste their flavour as
I try and place what sound used to feel like.

I can feel the inside, the outside is slow to catch up.
Everything is so slow and yet I can't keep up,
I try and turn my head, force my lips to part,
but I cannot control what used to be mine and before
I can speak, their hands are moving me and
the memory of touch sears through my body and I am
heaving.

Every muscle screams out to me, stretch,
but the voice of the body before me is flowing
through my bloodstream, ringing in my ears
and in this moment I can't place if it is language or

blood that I am gagging on.

I want to hear what my blood is telling me,
but there are men with skin,
in white coats and masks inches from my face and
all I hear is the
fear in their eyes.

I am starting to panic, I've forgotten how to breathe,
I'm trapped, I'm trying to take flight,
little voice in the centre of me,
close your eyes.

I am weightless, light as air,
complete and whole in this form,
I am,
unknowing,
remembering the
known, and
I am laughing.

She is holding my hand and
in the centre of my self at the
same time and I am peaceful.

I am floating and trying to make
sense of here and there and
there.
We are surrounded by
stars, I imagine being
a star and
I am burning with something.

I come
and go and come
and go and
I am lost
in many places.

Conscious,
unconscious,
I am solid, stone in
flesh form and
I am tiny pieces
scattered in the
night sky.

I feel like Alice,
falling down the rabbit hole,
only I am Alice,
and the rabbit,
and the hole and
I am the Mad Hatter
hysterical when it
dawns on me, I am
in all things.

Everything is blinding,
opening my eyes and
keeping them open is a
struggle and every time I
let them fall, I am hoping
to fly, but it is intermittent
and not nearly as often as
I am asking for.

He approaches me slowly,
but it is lightning speed and
I am flying from the bed to
avoid him, to escape the
needle he is trying to imbed
into me and all I can taste is
the blood that came before this,
making a home of my veins
and I am screaming.

I feel him consciously enforce a
calm tone, but his energy is
not calm and the racing of his heart
is loud in my ear, the vibration of his
mood, filling the room and this is the only
language I hear now. He glances
at the clock, my terror an
inconvenience and I am surrounded
by foreign beings
but I am the alien.

They feed me heavy medication,
their remedy for the shakes, the
ache, the weight and I am dizzy.

Everything is loud and the
vibration of my own voice is
deafening.

My shoulders are mountains,
buckling and I break from
this prison.

I am in motion, travelling backward
at the speed of light into my
past selves and I am dying deaths
I never knew I died.

I am lying naked, flat on my back in a room I
do not recognise and I am remembering how
hard, solid feels.
I am listening and trying not to listen,
a thousand sounds invading me and I cannot
place them, I cannot
shut them out.
A high pitched beeping shoots
through me and buries itself inside of me and
my skin is crawling.
I am moaning from the pressure in my ears that
travels into the centre of my brain and I am
retching.

There are waves inside of me, blood
lapping its way through my limbs, I am
trapped in this skin and I am begging
them not to touch me.

My tongue keeps getting twisted though
and I am gagging on it when people
enter the room.

Psyche surprises me,
this is your family and I
stare up at them, searching for
what's familiar, but
nothing is.

Lady in the corner, stands,
approaches me, attempts to
sling the thin sheet over my
naked body and I groan at the

thought, push her away and lay
naked as the day I was born,
a single touch sending agony
rippling through me.

When I next open my eyes, it is dark
and I am grateful for it.
A faint light is glowing
from the corner of the room and I
gasp when I
see her.

I am awestruck, she is levitating
beside the baby I cannot reach for and
she is pure light, singing.

She doesn't face me, but she passes
thoughts from herself and I
understand.

Lady in the corner is oblivious,
scribbles on her paper, does
not notice my body jolting, does not
witness the silent tears rolling down my
cheeks, nor the joy in my body
barely breathing.

Days that last for years are
swallowing me, I am present and
not present.
When the woman made of
light, is near I am
calmer but when I cannot find
her in my vision my chest rises and
falls rapidly and they don't leave me
like I want them to.

My baby is a metre from me, the
separation is unbearable and on
the forty eighth hour I heave my body
up and I am sitting.

The motion is too fast, everything is
sharp and I am spinning.
Pain is searing through me, lady in the corner
passes fragile small one to me and I
look down at the star wrapped in skin
in my arms.
I slowly sweep my hand over the
full head of hair
that gave me life and
Heaven is right here.

People are driving me home, people that
love me and have spent years learning to
know me, but I have changed in seven days
and my lips are stuck together with a glue of
confusion and I am a bird huddled, staring
out the window, a quivering mixture of bliss
and distress.

I cry the whole way home and
they ask me why but my mouth
can't remember
how to turn itself inside
out to lie, truth is flowing
like a waterfall from my lips
and nobody knows this language.

I feel like an
infant,
learning to walk, to
talk with lips that speak a different
language to my tongue and
frustration bites me, rage
escaping me, hurt flying from
my fingertips and my throat in
a whole array of ways that
don't even closely,
resemble Love and I despise
the Me I have returned to.

The adjusting is everlasting.

I'm lying on the soil,
screaming at the sky,
it's wet and the smell of the
deep earth is filling my lungs with
remembering.

Voice behind my eyelids reminds me,
you are already every element
in physical form.

The time I spend
recovering, is
misshapen.
I am a lamb in lion form,
a supernova, caged.
I am a mist, bodied and
shackled, ready to
shed this skin and every
layer peels back a new
unknowing.

The flashbacks are incessant.
I am losing touch with me and
myself and I don't know what's
real anymore.

It feels like I'm dreaming but I
never wake up, just keep
tumbling over thin air and catching
my breath with the fright.

Other peoples' faces are inches from
my own and I can smell their
intentions.

Their thoughts are
loud in the centre of my head and
I am disorientated, a flower
blown from its stem, flailing everywhere.

Later, they tell me it was a 'moment'
and I can feel my face speaking for
me, no effort to conceal my confusion,
my wonder.
I am asking myself, how a moment
can be eternal and 'time' is an
old word, that I thought I knew,
but like a disloyal lover, I have
uncovered the truth and everything
makes sense, but not like it used to.

I lock myself away in a
tower of my making,
an entire spectrum of
human emotion drowning me
and I am choking on the feelings
it was quiet to not feel.

I am all rage, anger is a
flavour that imbeds itself
into my taste buds and I
can't spit it out.

I am a god dressed in
skin, fully
aware of my own
otherworldliness and I am
lonely, so terribly lonely, my own
kind, lost in an
amnesia I have left behind
and I am craving home.

I am alone in a small space,
my cheeks are damp, cold but all
I feel is the deep throbbing of
severance.

I spend eternities dissociating,
aimlessly wandering my own psyche,
looking for unfamiliar faces that might
awaken my memory and it is
so
excruciatingly
quiet.

I cannot stand it.

My throat is hoarse,
I have been singing for days,
attempting to replicate a
sound I've never heard, a
sound that is burned into
me with remembering.

I am longing for the
music. I am a baby crying for
my mother and woman of
light, appears, graces me with her
presence and hums,
Om.

I am deserted in a foreign place,
with a message
and a tongue
that has been split in two,
that is numb beneath
its own weight,
that knows every word by heart,
in a language no one else is speaking.

Rachel Finch

I cry for an age,
she returns to me and the
sight of her wings fill me with a
breath I never need
exhale.

Her voice is a caterpillar that
cocoons itself within me,

every time it stirs,
remember,
every
time
it
stirs,
remember
who
you
are.

The days are long and cold,
the tremors are unending and I am
complaining to the
deepest part of myself.
She is not quiet,
the evolving is an unfolding
and I am origami in the wind.

It is nightfall and I
have been waiting. I am
buzzing from the inside out.
counting breaths,
counting backwards,
counting each flutter of
my eyes beneath their lids
and I am patient.

The practice was long,
frustrating, but she has
shown me and I am rising,
oblivious to everything but
the gentle hum of my shifting
and I am bursting from this skin
and birthing wings.

I am running along the shore
chasing stars and I am trying to
take flight.
The storm brings heavy winds and
I am relishing this feeling.
I let my eyes close softly and I don't care
if I trip, I tell myself,
the fall will take me down and down
is up in another place.

The sea is crashing beside me,
the sound elating,
I feel every goose bump rise to meet me
in this seeking.

In my mind, I am in a tunnel,
surrounded by hundreds of me
and I know my way.

I am smiling and
she
is laughing and
we
are exhilarated.

She feeds me gratification,
they can never take this.

She is liquid gold, she is
flowing down into me, into a
new mould, she is filling every
atom of my being with sacred
truth and she is burying herself
in every heart chamber.

Rachel Finch

She tells me,
kiss their wounds
the way the galaxies
kissed yours and
let every bruise
know this love.

She is my instinct and my instinct is
no longer a whisper,
loud in my ear as he lies
through his teeth,
she is insistent,
untruth.

And I love him through
his brokenness and I
love him through his
healing and I love him
with the love of a
sky that knows his
secrets and it is
the purest thing I have ever
done.

In a crowd of people,
I am cattle, I am
herded and I hate it.
Everybody's faces look
the same and the outside
hides the inside and it
bothers me.

She tells me,
you will recognise them when you
see them, you will know the
glow around their outer form and
you will know their voice by
the sound of the same star.

Baby girl with the
full head of hair
is 87cm tall,
with vocal chords
that sound like harps
and a tongue full of
all the right words.

I have kept my knowings
hidden.
I am tongue twisters and
riddles and I sing to her
so I don't tumble
my thoughts out my mouth.

I am astonished, when
she casually asks me,
"Remember when I was your Mummy,
and you were the child?"
I am ice cold.
"Remember when I chose you as
my Mummy?"
I am slowing down.
"You remember, don't you Mummy,
when we lived in the other house and
I was a boy?"
And I am hurtling through space,
299,792 kilometres per second
and
I remember.

Everywhere I turn, there are
shadows.
I have become afraid, of
my own shadow, of
my own reflection,
a corpse,
that stares into me with
empty eyes and a peculiar
expression.
The un-illuminated disturb me
and I am praying to the
moon and she says,
use your voice to shine
light in a
dark place.

I like the shower, because the shower
drowns out the deafening silence.

In the rushing stream I hear her,
find your courage,
to live your best life,
to let go of lack,
to do what you were
born to do.

I am sitting at my father's deathbed,
tears streaming down my face,
listening to the
singing no one else hears and the
knowing
and the
agony
and the
elation
are exquisite.

Heavy heart,
heavier, I can't stop
the floodgates.
I am
all knowing,
I am
all accepting,
I am
all understanding,
still my heart shatters
beneath the weight.
She says,
the growing pain is the ascension,
use your magic and align.

It has been a thousand days,
a thousand lifetimes, since I
have seen his face,
heard his voice,
felt his warmth and I am
lying motionless,
an inch above my body,
binaural beats vibrating
through me and she takes me
to him.

I am silent witness to a moment
in time and I am invisible.
She holds my hand and I feel
her stare fixed on
who I am in
this moment
but I am mesmerised.

He is angelic
and my soul
swells with this
enormous feeling.

He is dressed in a white suit,
white trilby to match and I can
feel what he feels rippling
through me. I know he
feels a million dollars,
looks it too.

He is laughing and this
sound echoes into me.

I am a million sparks
of electricity and I ignite.

He is sitting on the moon and
the moon is a crescent
beneath him and a whole
beside him and the
illumination is breathtaking
when he looks my way and I
see the birth of the universe in
the pupil of his eye.

Light rests on my lips and
I want to form it into words
but the memory overwhelms
me and all I am is smiles and
heavy sobs.

She is an oracle,
that tells me Heaven's secrets,
that hands me my future then
hides it, tells me to go seek it and
loves me through my mystery.

They have wronged this body, they have
tied me up and hung me, they have
broken this skin and the bleeding is
a sacred act, she whispers,
forgive them
and I'm already crying tears of
absolution, deep in a black hole,
remembering,
reliving, my own mercy.

I am familiar with her
presence and the
sound without sound of
her voice.

I travel with her in my
dreams, I travel with her in
my waking hours, we
reminisce and when she
flies me through a rainbow
I am every colour of the
spectrum, lost in light.

I am watching the smoke
rise and I am
one with the flame.

I am sage and berries,
waves and riddles and I
will never unknow her.

I am deep in the forest and she
is teaching me.
She tells me,
look for the patterns
and my eyes are searching
the trees for a message.

Raven flies past me,
turns around,
perches on a fallen branch,
cocks his head and speaks to me.

Wind blows, rustles every leaf
from its toes, whispers into my
open ears and speaks to me.

Twilight creeps upon us,
carrying the moon,
a soft illuminating glow,
shedding light on all my
dark parts and speaks to me.

Earth is her chorus,
you are a force of nature,
you are in all things.

I wake to the sun and
she wakes to me and
we both give life and
burn.

I am a billion moments,
in a billion places,
with a billion names,
none that I recognise but
Holy.

I am deep in
meditation,
she meets me in
my soul and
tells me,
we are clearing,
I am vibrating,
we are releasing,
I am pulsating
we are rising,
so rise.
I inhale and
I am up.

They think I'm lost
inside my head, but
I am nowhere close.

I am light years away
in a sky that folds
to my bend, that
moulds itself into me
and I am levitating in
a paradise of
constellation castles.

I am flying,
wingless,
I am a beam
of light,
shimmering.

I am looking into a
transparent sphere and
I am looking at the Me
I used to be.

I am watching myself
crumpled in a corner,
drowning in a pool of
my own salt water and
the reliving is a remembering
when she tells me,
the breaking is the birthing.

Spirit is within every form
and I am loving
petals like limbs.

Fear is an old word,
from a previous life,
in a language I don't
speak anymore.

Courage is a new word,
in a new tongue,
that sits itself between
my shoulder blades and
hums.

They showed me a
thousand new feelings
and never told me the
words to name them.
I am swimming in the
quiet awareness of
feelings with no name.

I carried a story for twelve years,
let it sit in my heart and teach
and then release itself.

Sit the ocean in a glass
by your temple.
Soak it into your aura.
Let it cleanse, let it
renew.

My tongue is a
supernova and I am
all gratitude.

Thank you,
Thank you,
Thank you.

And you
and you
and you
and you
and you
and you
are made of Light.

You are a body of flesh,
a brook of blood.
You are an essence of
consciousness, a stream
of truth and love.
You are all contradictions,
an enigma, and you are
beautiful.

I was born April 2nd 1986,
I died and was reborn, June 2nd 2006
and I came back not of before.

I came back a castle and the ivy that
dresses it. I came back a bear and
the honey that laces its lips. I came
back a woman with memories of
other lives, a witch, the stake and the
flames. I came back a newborn,
unable to cry, a wave, every flower,
a borrowed kiss. I came back, every
sound in the flesh, a billion tears, a
trillion laughs, a peacock's feather.
I came back the blood drenching the
lion's jaw, the final breath of the zebra's life,
a grasshopper, a seahorse, a bird in the sky,
every twilight, every memory ever made.

And I am still stunned.
And it is all worth it.
And it is all beautiful.

The blood pumping through my body murmurs,
a quiet voice to prompt the recollection,

You are Love, You are Love, You are Love.

HOW LUCKY AM I TO HAVE TASTED LIGHT
AND STILL REMEMBER THE FLAVOUR.

RACHEL | BRUISED BUT NOT BROKEN

About The Author

Rachel Finch is a UK based writer that originally started using poetry as a way to accurately express herself after a number of traumatic experiences in her young life. She is the founder of the online community Bruised But Not Broken which was started with the purpose to raise awareness of abuse and trauma and to provide a place of comfort and support throughout the healing process. She firmly believes that it was with the support of this community that she was able to recover from sexual abuse. Rachel is mother to four young children and dedicates her time to her family and to guiding others on their own healing journey.

You can connect with Rachel on Facebook and WordPress under Bruised But Not Broken.

Made in the USA
Middletown, DE
22 May 2019